Eighth-Note Rock and Beyond

By Glenn Ceglia with Dom Famularo

Music Engraving, Layout, and Book Design
by Joe Bergamini, Jesse Robbins & Amanda Grimaldi

Edited by
Joe Bergamini

Cover Design: Michele Heusel

Front Cover Drawing: Steve Leahy

Photo of Author: Karl Ermisch

Original Cover Design and Layout: Michelle Sarafin

Layout and Editing Assistance: Chris Clemente and Willie Rose

Additional Editing: Dave Black

For downloadable play-along songs, please visit
www.musiclearningcurve.com

WIZDOM MEDIA PUBLICATIONS
PO Box 45, Whippany, NJ 07981 USA

Copyright © 2007 by Wizdom Media LLC
All Rights Reserved.

Exclusively distributed by
Alfred Publishing Co., Inc.

Table of Contents

Key

About the Authors

Glenn Ceglia

Glenn Ceglia, originally from Long Island, has been an active drummer and music educator in upstate New York for over twenty years. He has earned an associate's degree in music from Nassau Community College, and bachelor's and master's degrees in music education from the Crane School of Music at SUNY Potsdam.

Glenn has had the privilege of studying drums with John Blowers, Ronnie Gould, Charles Perry and Jim Petercsak. Since 2001, Glenn has been studying with Dom Famularo who has not only brought him to a whole new playing level, but has been an incredible inspiration as an educator.

About the Authors

Dom Famularo

His sensational drumming and brilliant communication skills have earned Dom Famularo a reputation of being the world's leading motivational drumset artist and educator. Through history-making tours of China and the Far East, and with standing ovations to capacity audiences at virtually every major drumming event in Europe and the Americas, this vibrant performer from Long Island, New York is renowned for delivering entertaining and awe-inspiring performances unlike any other.

Tutored by legendary greats Joe Morello, Jim Chapin, Al Miller, and Ronnie Benedict, Dom combines the masterful techniques of the past with the parameter-pushing concepts of the present for a highly creative and uniquely personal style of drumming. With hands powered by the famous Moeller technique and feet dancing through high-speed, double-pedal bass drumming patterns, he delivers performances that dip and dive through dynamics and styles with energy and ease. Elements of jazz, funk, fusion, and Latin rhythms permeate his sound, while every stroke speaks to the inventiveness that makes his drumming so exciting, entertaining, and inspiring.

The first Western drummer to perform clinics in China, Dom is accustomed to making headlines. He was a special guest performer at the first-ever Buddy Rich Tribute Concert, an event which he helped organize. He was a highlight as host and performer at the Pacific Rim Drum Invitational (the first drum event to be simulcast live on the Internet), and he's a primary attraction at star-studded drumming events such as the Koblenz International Drummer Meeting in Germany, the Florida Drum Expo, the Paris Music Show, the massive Drummers Day in Australia, the Heartbeat World Rhythm spectacle for Canadian TV, and the Montreal Drumfest.

Dom doesn't rely on major band affiliations as a claim to fame, but performances with the Buddy Rich Big Band, B.B. King, Lionel Hampton, Chuck Leavell (Rolling Stones), T Lavitz (the Dixie Dregs), and the Louie Bellson Big Band reveal the pedigree of his playing. He has shared the stage with Dave Weckl, Steve Gadd, Vinnie Colaiuta, Simon Phillips, Billy Cobham, Bernard Purdie, Rod Morgenstein, Chester Thompon, Terry Bozzio, Will Calhoun, Deen Castronovo, Russ McKinnon, Chad Smith, Mark Schulman, Denny Carmassi, Liberty DeVitto and Jim Chapin in worldwide drumming events. Dom fondly remembers performances with both Jeff Porcaro and Larrie Londin, both of whom he is proud to have had a chance to meet and perform with.

In addition to large drumming expos and clinic tours, Dom is an active educator at colleges, drum schools and camps. He has performed at the Percussive Arts Society Convention (PASIC), Percussion Institute of Technology (PIT) in Los Angeles, Berklee College of Music in Boston, The Collective in New York, KOSA Camp in Vermont, North Texas State University, and Extreme Drummers Camp at the Modern Music School in Germany. In addition, he is an in-demand consultant to major music corporations, and serves as Education Director for Sabian Ltd., Vic Firth, Inc., Mapex drums and Evans drumheads.

Dom was voted Best Clinician by the readers of *Modern Drummer* magazine in 2005 and 2006, and by the readers of *DRUM!* in 2006. He is also the author of *It's Your Move* (Alfred Publications).

Visit Dom's websites at: www.domfamularo.com and www.myspace.com/domfamularo.

Foreword

I am always impressed with honest dedication to our art form. As a player and as a teacher, Glenn Ceglia is a great example of conviction to learning and honesty in sharing this knowledge and experience with everyone.

For some years, Glenn has been traveling over 500 miles to study with me—what a zest he shows for learning! He has made dramatic musical changes, and he has inspired me.

His desire to write a clear learning process for beginning drumset students speaks volumes about his enthusiasm to assist others to have fun. *Eighth-Note Rock and Beyond* is the result of his effort to spread the message: Have fun with drumming!

The book is clear and takes you on an organized path to playing rock. I really like the counts under each groove—they really guide the student. You can use these beats to play with any of your favorite songs.

Follow the book, play the beats, and mostly—have fun!

—Dom Famularo

About the Book

Eighth-Note Rock and Beyond was designed to teach basic beats commonly used in rock music. After twenty years of teaching drums in the public school system, I wrote this book to prepare my students for other, more advanced, rock books. This book was designed with the beginning drumset student in mind, but may be used by any drummer. To develop good hand technique and prepare for the rhythms in this book, I recommend that beginning drum students first complete an elementary snare drum method. There are many good ones available—the appendix of this book offers some suggestions in this and other areas.

Eighth-Note Rock and Beyond is a sequence of eighth-note based rock beats that I developed by observing my students, and determining what made a beat easy or difficult to master. It is not mandatory to follow the sequence exactly—students and teachers may decide to alter the sequence to accommodate individual learning differences.

1. The book starts with a rhythmic counting key.
2. Throughout this book you will find the straight eighth-note rock hi-hat pattern. Once you feel successful with the eighth-note hi-hat pattern, the variation patterns on pages 12 - 13 may be used.
3. Chapter 1 introduces basic beats with quarter notes and eighth notes.
4. Chapter 2 uses beats with four bass drum sixteenth notes in preparation for sixteenth-note variation patterns in chapters three through nine.
5. Chapters 3 through 9 focus on sixteenth-note variation patterns.
6. Chapter 9 combines rhythms from chapters 1 through 8 and introduces ghost notes on the snare drum.

While working on this book, you should set aside some listening time. Listen to rock music from the 1950s to the present. Also, listen to other styles of music that happened before rock music, such as early forms of jazz (swing, Dixieland, big band), and especially blues, which is the style of music that led directly to rock. You will be surprised at how many rock drumming ideas date back to these earlier eras. In his DVD, *Drumset Technique/History of the U.S. Beat*, Steve Smith does an excellent job of presenting drumset history and styles. You will see and hear how drumset players developed the straight eighth-note style so commonly used in rock music. I also advise that students subscribe to *Modern Drummer* magazine, and watch drum videos, DVD's, and live performances.

This book was not written as a study in hand or foot technique; however, I recommend studying the techniques discussed in "How to Use This Book" on the next page. (See the appendix for studies on the Moeller stroke, free stroke, open-handed playing, cross-over technique, and foot technique.)

How to Use This Book

1. Use the counting system in this book. Notes are written in bold; rests are not. Hi-hat counting appears above the notes; bass and snare counting appears below the notes.

2. All the beats in this book have three parts: 1) hi-hat (H.H.), written on the space above the staff; 2) snare drum (S.D.), written on the third space; and 3) bass drum (B.D.), written on the first space.

3. When the student is comfortable playing the H.H. part as written, try playing the H.H. part on the ride cymbal. Then, add the hi-hat patterns played with the foot (see page 8).

4. To develop equal control in all limbs, each chapter should be played using both the cross-over technique and the open-handed technique. The cross-over technique is so-named because the player's stronger hand crosses over to play the hi-hat while the weaker hand plays the snare drum. Open-handed playing is the reverse; the player's weaker hand plays the hi-hat and the stronger hand plays the snare drum. If you have two hi-hats, one on the left and one on the right (auxiliary), you can use the auxiliary hi-hat for the lead hand instead of crossing over (see appendix for examples of the techniques mentioned above).

5. The majority of this book features accented snare drum notes on beats two and four. To play the accented two and four back beats on the snare drum, students should use a technique called the Moeller stroke. If you and your teacher are not familiar with the Moeller stroke, please purchase a copy of the book *It's Your Move* by Dom Famularo with Joe Bergamini, and the Jim Chapin video *Speed, Power, Control, Endurance*. I also recommend studying with a teacher who teaches the Moeller stroke which will enable you to see live demonstrations of the technique and also immediately help with your efforts. A few drumset artists that use the Moeller technique are Jim Chapin, Joe Morello, Steve Gadd, David Garibaldi, Dom Famularo, Will Calhoun, Stewart Copland, Kenny Arnoff, Steve Smith, Vinnie Colaiuta, Dave Weckl, Dennis Chambers, Gregg Bissonette, Gene Krupa, Buddy Rich, Jeff Porcaro, and Larrie Londin. Watch videos featuring these artists and you will see the Moeller technique in use. To see the Moeller stroke performed by Dom Famularo, go to www.domfamularo.com and download his free cyberlessons.

6. While playing the hi-hat with either hand you will use either the Moeller stroke or the technique known as the free stroke. If you are not familiar with the free stroke refer to *It's Your Move* and the Joe Morello video *The Natural Approach to Technique*. Also, see Dom Famularo perform the free stroke on his web site. A few drumset artists that use the "Free Stroke" technique are Joe Morello, Steve Gadd, David Garibaldi, Dom Famularo, Terry Bozzio, Simon Phillips, Vinnie Colaiuta, Steve Smith, Dennis Chambers, Gregg Bissonette, Chester Thompson, Phil Collins, Virgil Donati, John Blackwell, Gene Krupa, Buddy Rich, John Bonham, Jeff Porcaro, and Larrie Londin. If you learn the Moeller stroke and free stroke, it will help you develop a natural, relaxed drumset technique for playing all styles of drumset music.

7. For stick grip I recommend playing matched grip and having a qualified professional drum teacher show you how to hold and use a pair of drum sticks correctly. There is no substitute for a great teacher.

8. Play with a sense of commitment and passion when playing each beat in this book. As with any rock drum book or rock song, you need to give 100% for even the most simplistic beat.

9. The final word for this book is *fun*. Even when you are working hard at a technique or beat, remember to have fun—you are playing the drums!

***

Other books from Wizdom Media Publications that work in conjunction with this book include:

It's Your Move by Dom Famularo and Joe Bergamini
Open-Handed Playing by Claus Hessler and Dom Famularo
Pedal Control by Dom Famularo and Joe Bergamini
The Weaker Side by Stephane Chamberland and Dom Famularo

Please check our web site, *wizdom-media.com*, for information about current and future releases.

About the CD

The included MP3 CD contains demonstrations of all the beats in the book. The tracks are set up so you can practice along with them. Each track begins with two bars of click, followed by four bars of the beat, followed by four bars of just click, followed by four more bars of the beat. The tracks are set up this way so you can hear yourself playing along with the correct beat, and then check yourself by playing along with just the click.

The track numbers on the CD correspond exactly with the exercise numbers in the book.

Counting Key

Counting is very important. Here is a counting key for the basic rhythm of each chapter.

Chapter 1

Chapter 2

Chapter 3

Chapter 4

Chapter 5

1 e + a 2 e + a 3 e + a 4 e + a   1 e + a 2 e + a 3 e + a 4 e + a

Chapter 6

1 e + a 2 e + a 3 e + a 4 e + a   1 e + a 2 e + a 3 e + a 4 e + a

Chapter 7

1 e + a 2 e + a 3 e + a 4 e + a   1 e + a 2 e + a 3 e + a 4 e + a

Chapter 8

1 e + a 2 e + a 3 e + a 4 e + a   1 e + a 2 e + a 3 e + a 4 e + a

Chapter 9

1 e + a 2 e + a 3 e + a 4 e + a   1 e + a 2 e + a 3 e + a 4 e + a

Hi-Hat/Ride Cymbal Variations

1. The following are hi-hat/ride variations using the rhythms contained in this book.
2. Once you are successful playing the beats as written, try the hi-hat/ride cymbal variations in which the hi-hat part is either played on the hi-hat or played on the ride cymbal (instead of the hi-hat).
3. These rhythms are suggestions—you are encouraged to also create your own patterns.

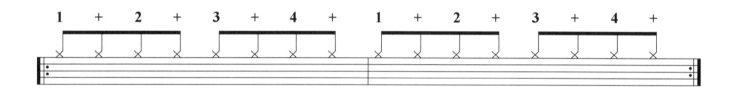

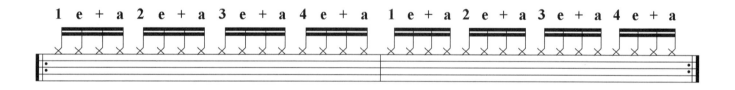

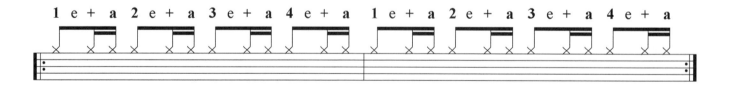

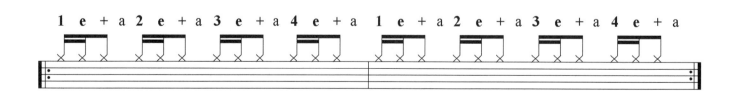

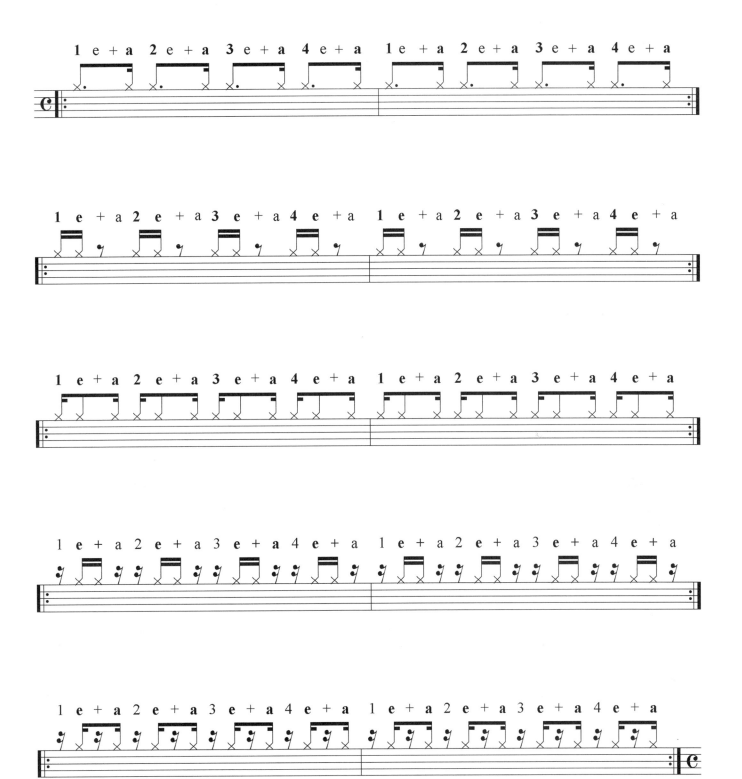

Hi-Hat Patterns Played with the Foot

1. When playing the ride cymbal, play the hi-hat with the foot by pressing the pedal down.
2. These patterns are suggestions. You are encouraged to also create your own patterns.

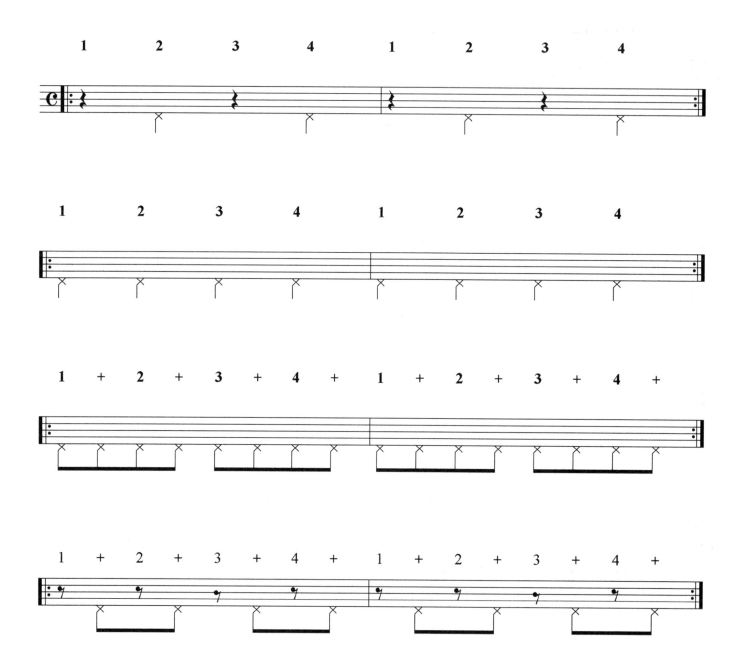

CHAPTER ONE

Rock Basics: Quarter-Note/Eighth-Note Combinations

1. This chapter is designed to establish the feeling of Eighth-Notes on the hi-hat while playing quarter notes and Eighth-Notes on the snare drum and bass drum.
2. To accent beats two and four, use the Moeller stroke.
3. MM marking = 88-144.

Warm-Up

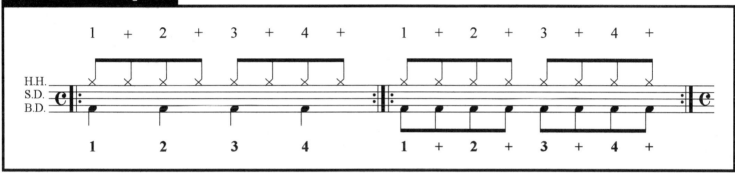

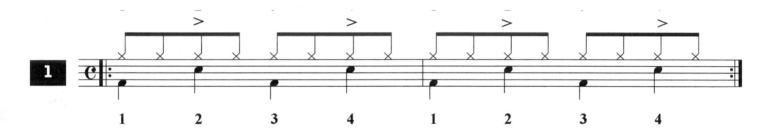

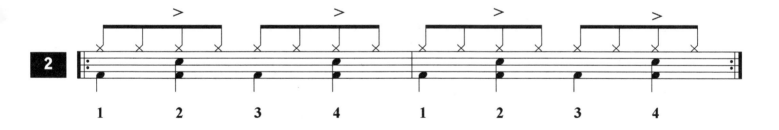

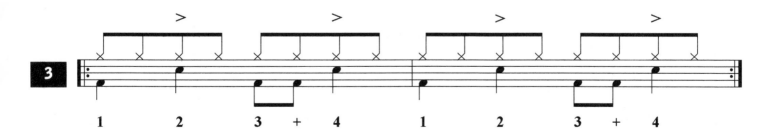

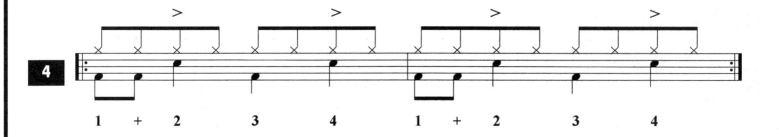

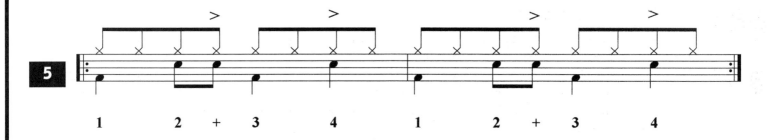

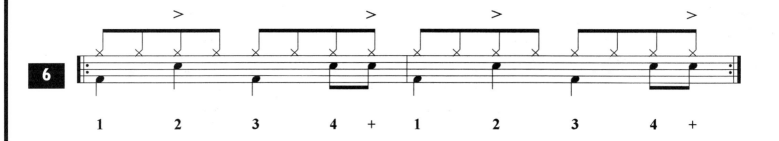

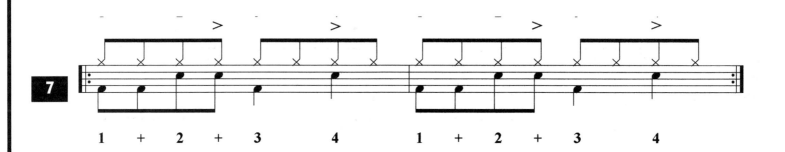

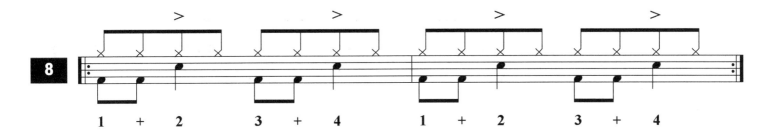

8

1 + 2   3 + 4   1 + 2   3 + 4

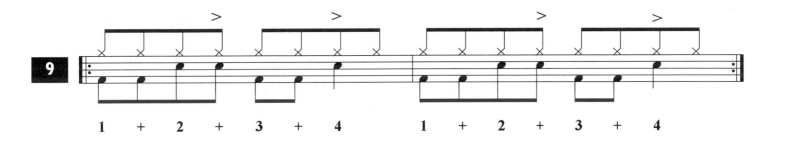

9

1 + 2 + 3 + 4   1 + 2 + 3 + 4

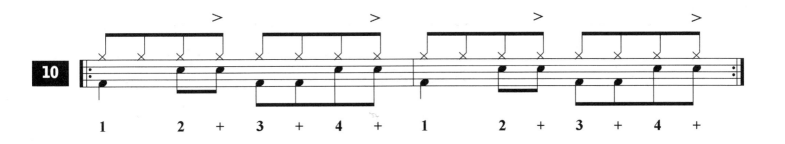

10

1   2 + 3 + 4 +   1   2 + 3 + 4 +

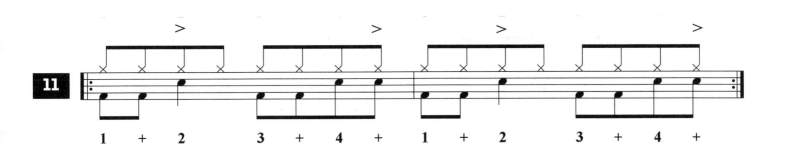

11

1 + 2   3 + 4 +   1 + 2   3 + 4 +

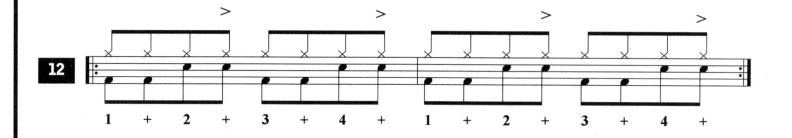

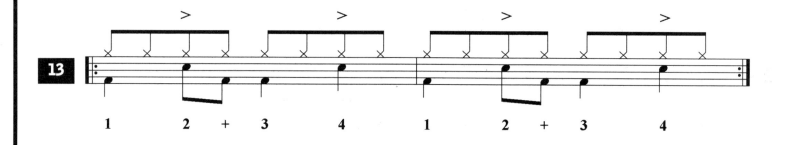

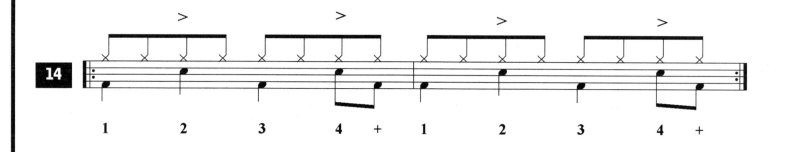

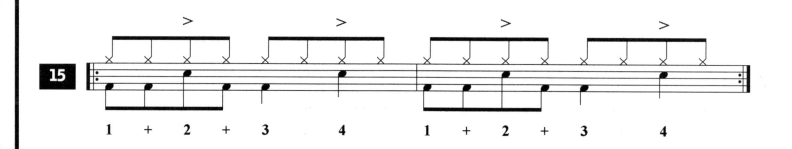

16

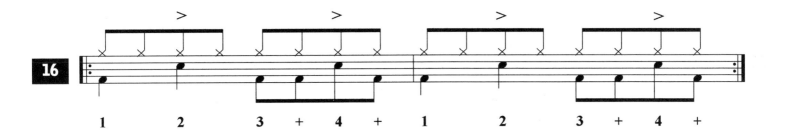

1   2   3 + 4 + 1   2   3 + 4 +

17

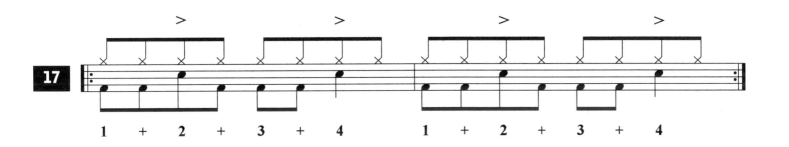

1 + 2 + 3 + 4   1 + 2 + 3 + 4

18

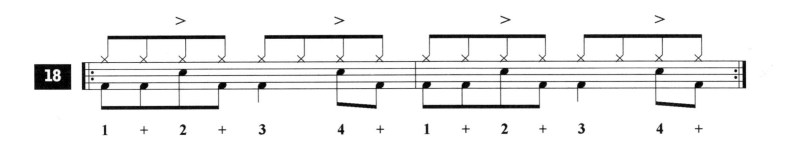

1 + 2 + 3   4 + 1 + 2 + 3   4 +

19

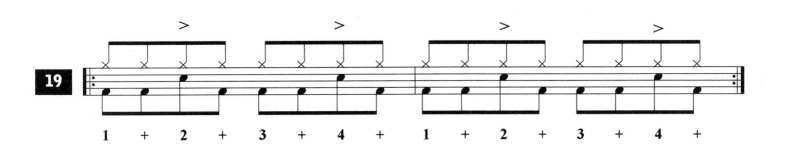

1 + 2 + 3 + 4 + 1 + 2 + 3 + 4 +

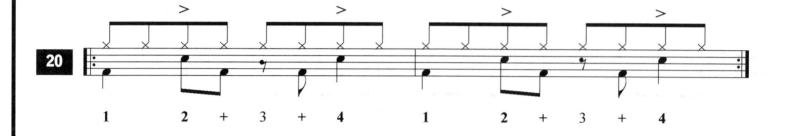

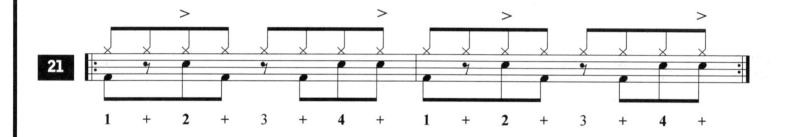

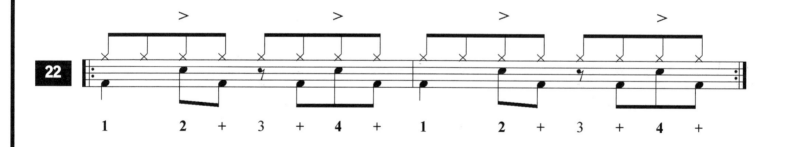

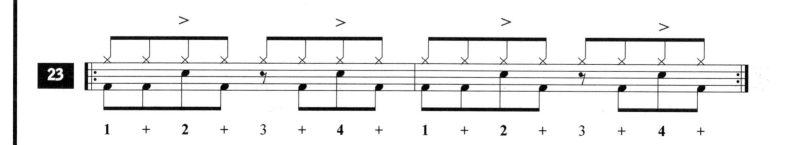

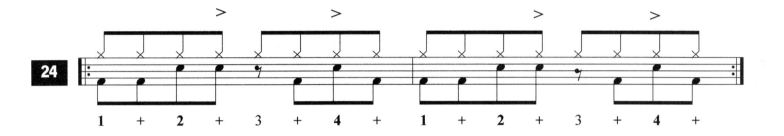

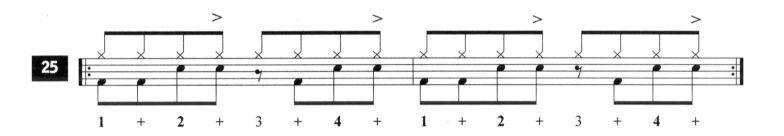

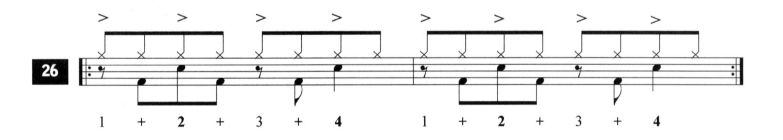

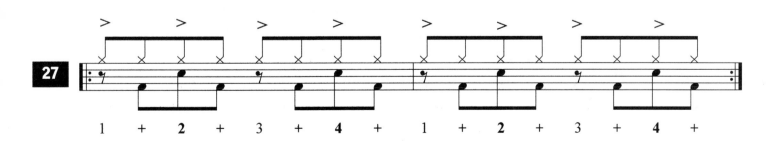

28

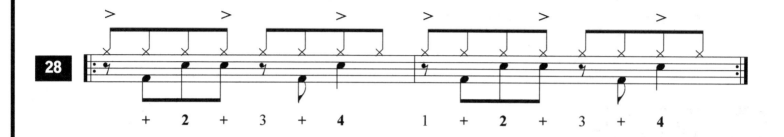

+ 2 + 3 + 4 1 + 2 + 3 + 4

29

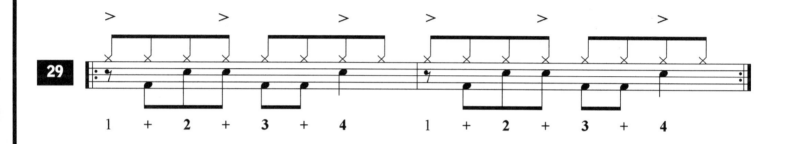

1 + 2 + 3 + 4 1 + 2 + 3 + 4

30

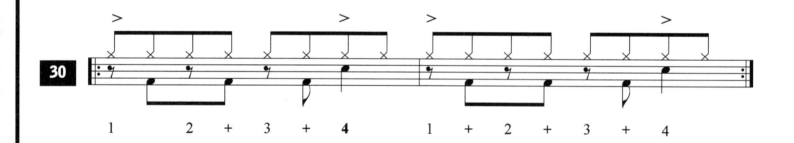

1 2 + 3 + 4 1 + 2 + 3 + 4

CHAPTER TWO
Four Sixteenth Notes on the Bass Drum

1. The goal is to learn sixteenth-note grooves in preperation for all sixteenth-note variations.
2. Speed is not the goal—work to make all beats line up.
3. Use the Moeller stroke to accent beats two and four.
4. MM marking = 88-100.

Warm-Up

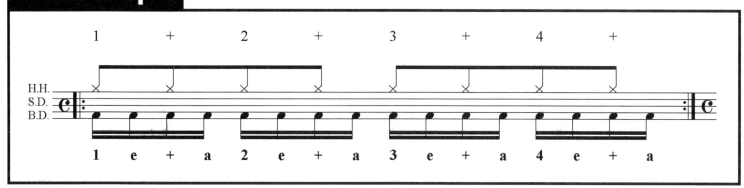

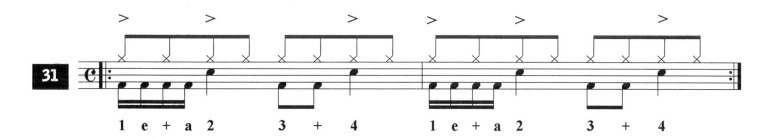

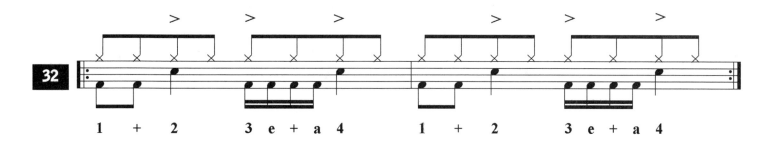

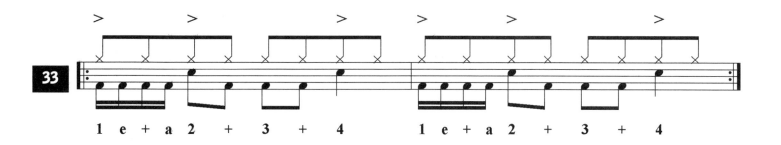

34

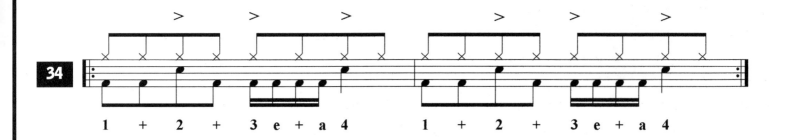

1 + 2 + 3 e + a 4   1 + 2 + 3 e + a 4

35

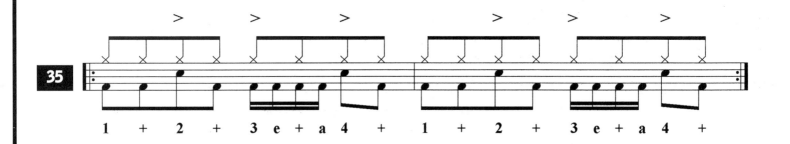

1 + 2 + 3 e + a 4 +   1 + 2 + 3 e + a 4 +

36

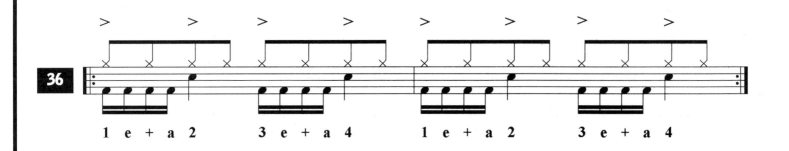

1 e + a 2   3 e + a 4   1 e + a 2   3 e + a 4

37

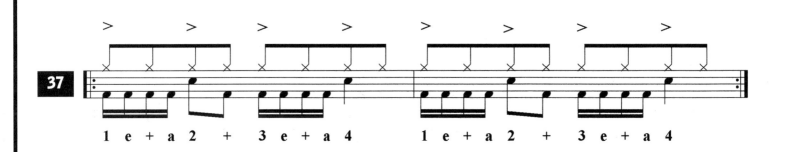

1 e + a 2 + 3 e + a 4   1 e + a 2 + 3 e + a 4

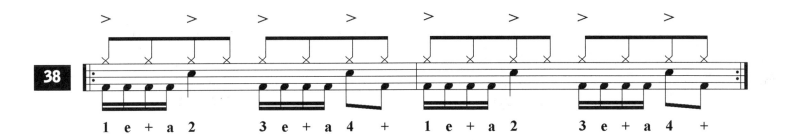

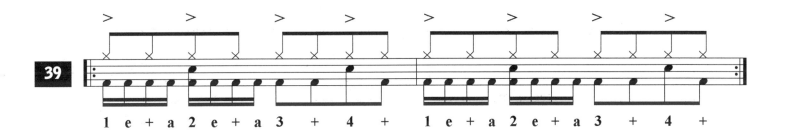

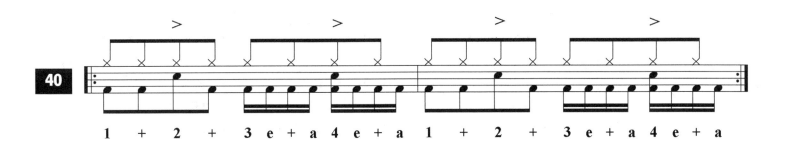

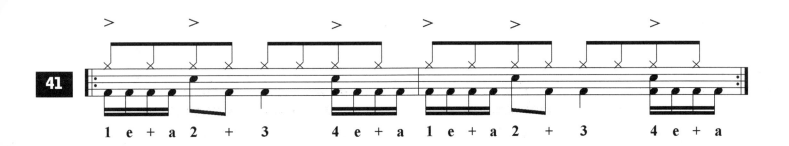

42

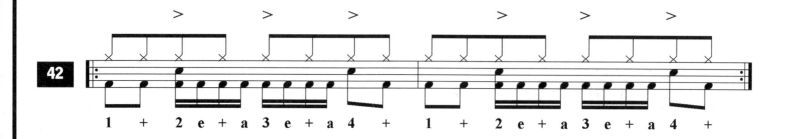

1 + 2 e + a 3 e + a 4 + 1 + 2 e + a 3 e + a 4 +

43

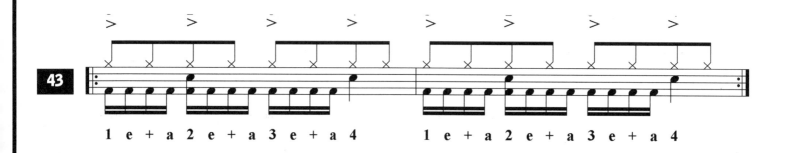

1 e + a 2 e + a 3 e + a 4 1 e + a 2 e + a 3 e + a 4

44

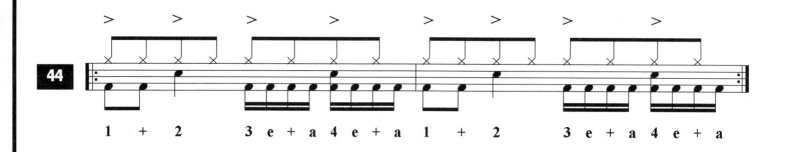

1 + 2 3 e + a 4 e + a 1 + 2 3 e + a 4 e + a

45

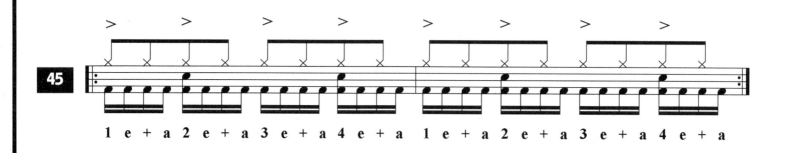

1 e + a 2 e + a 3 e + a 4 e + a 1 e + a 2 e + a 3 e + a 4 e + a

CHAPTER THREE
Adding the 8th/Two 16th Note-Pattern

1. These exercises add the 8th/Two 16th-note combination on the bass drum.
2. MM marking = 84-126.

Warm-Up

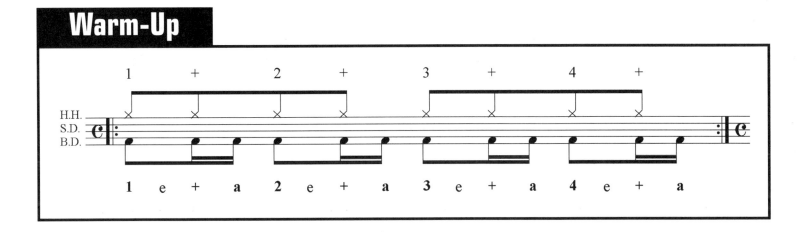

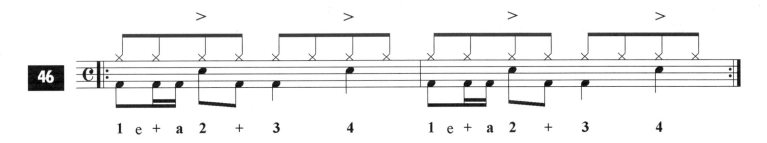

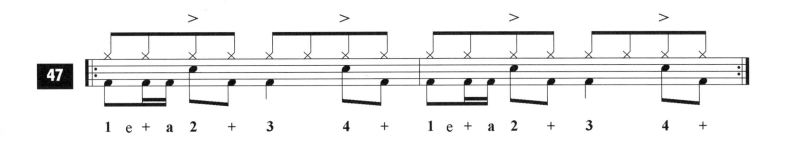

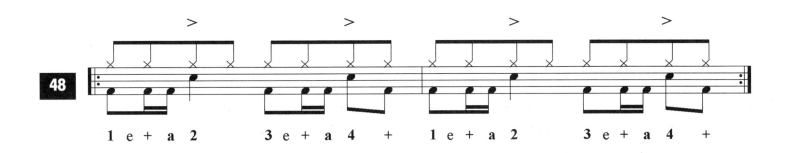

49

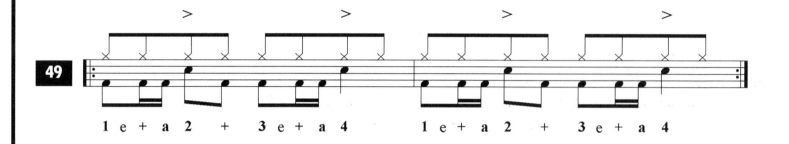

1 e + a 2 + 3 e + a 4   1 e + a 2 + 3 e + a 4

50

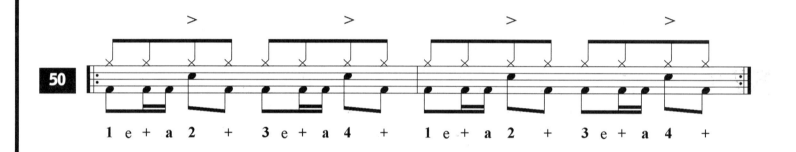

1 e + a 2 + 3 e + a 4 +   1 e + a 2 + 3 e + a 4 +

51

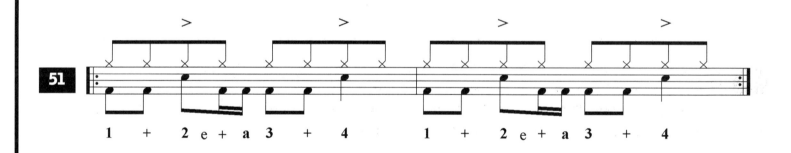

1 + 2 e + a 3 + 4   1 + 2 e + a 3 + 4

52

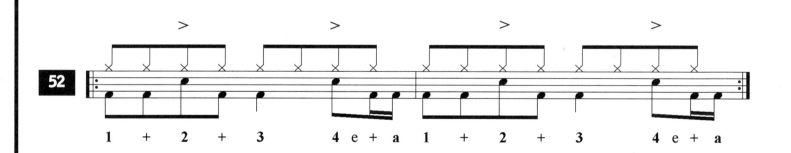

1 + 2 + 3   4 e + a 1 + 2 + 3   4 e + a

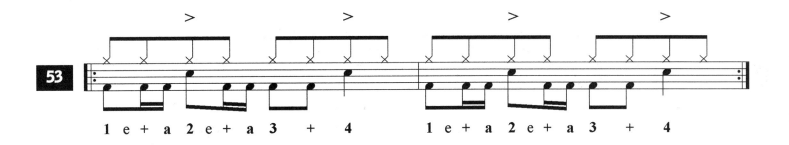

53

1 e + a 2 e + a 3 + 4   1 e + a 2 e + a 3 + 4

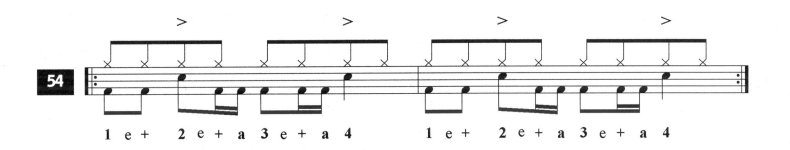

54

1 e + 2 e + a 3 e + a 4   1 e + 2 e + a 3 e + a 4

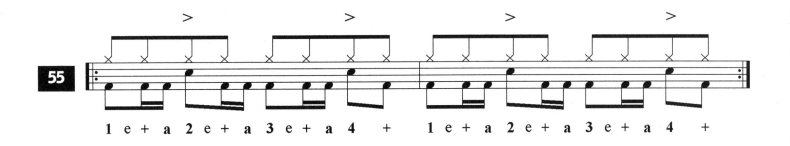

55

1 e + a 2 e + a 3 e + a 4 +   1 e + a 2 e + a 3 e + a 4 +

CHAPTER FOUR

Adding Two 16th/One 8th-Note Rhythmic Pattern

1. Adding the two 16th/8th-note rhythm.
2. Remember to use the counting key.
3. MM marking = 88-100.

Warm-Up

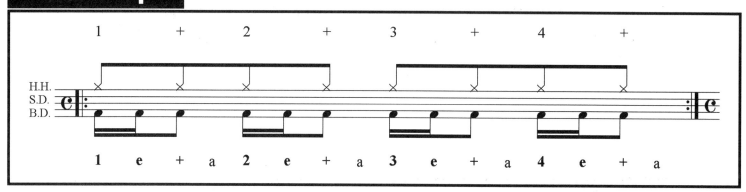

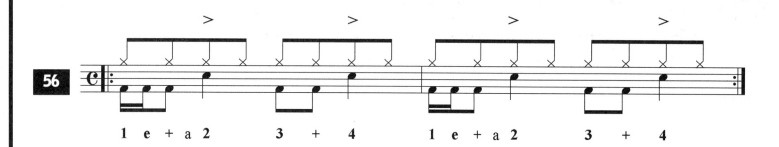

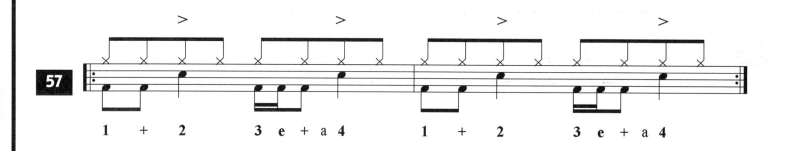

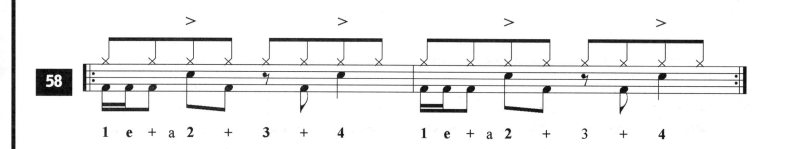

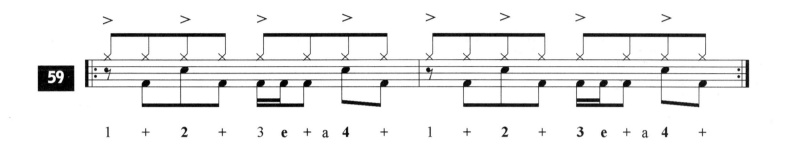

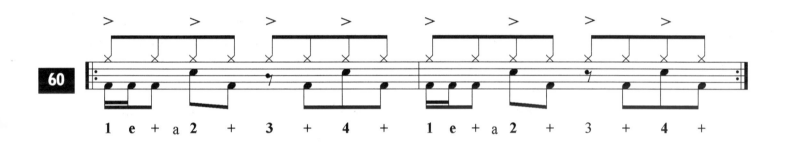

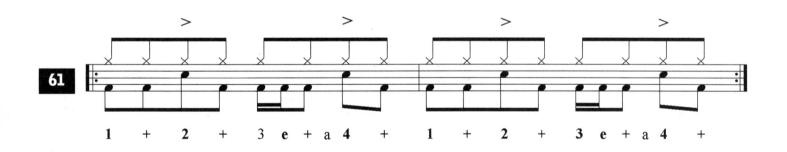

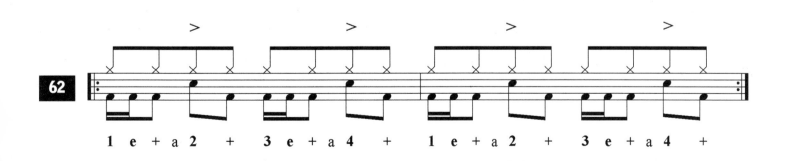

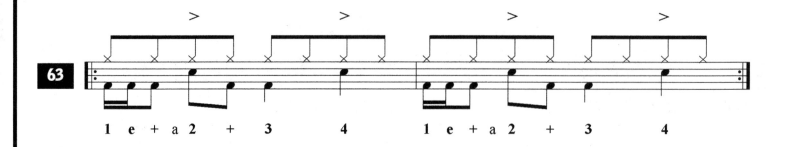

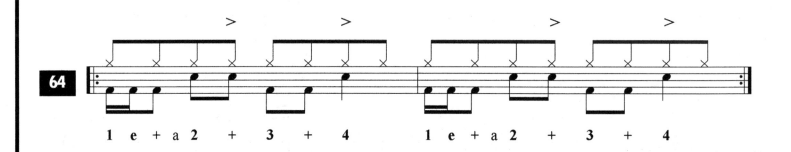

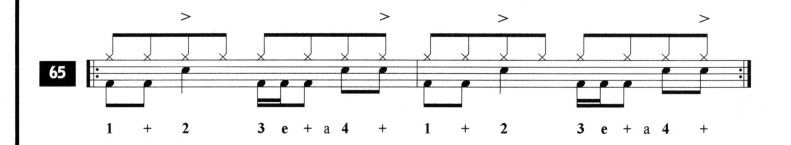

CHAPTER FIVE
Dotted 8th/16th-Note Rhythmic Pattern

1. Adding the dotted 8th/16th rhythm.
2. MM marking = 100-132.

Warm-Up

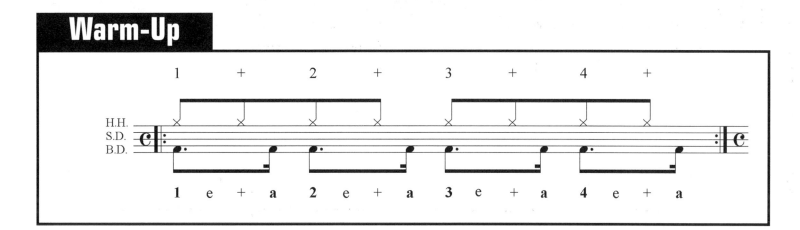

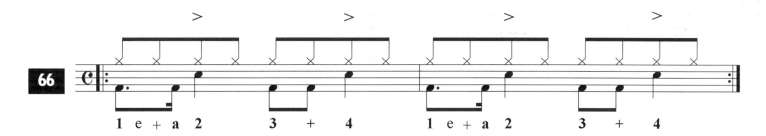

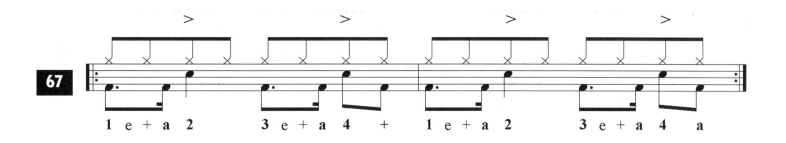

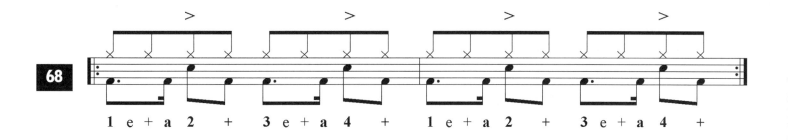

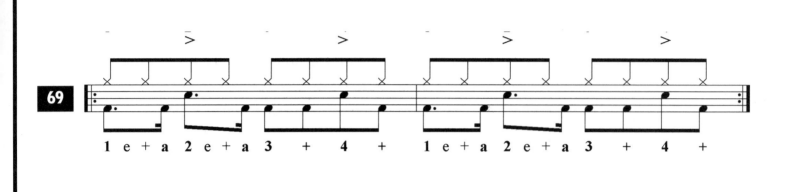

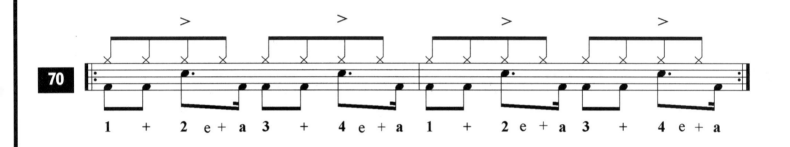

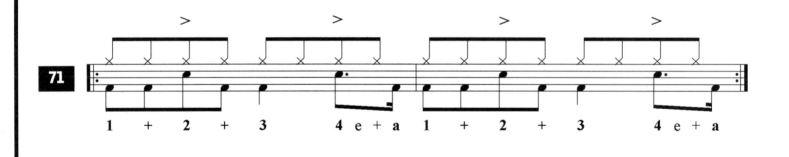

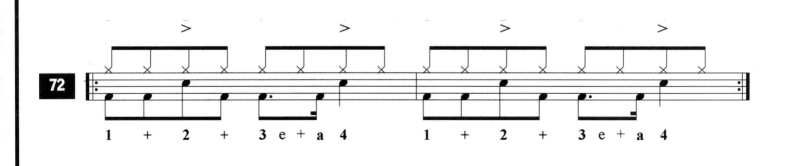

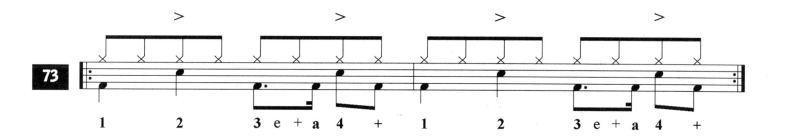

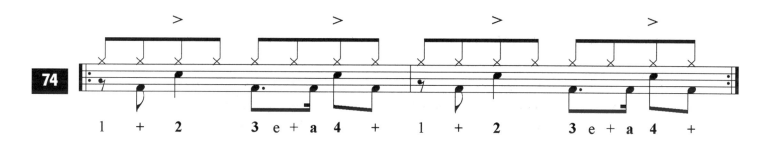

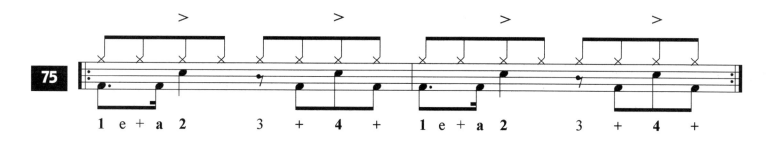

CHAPTER SIX
The Levee Bass Drum

1. Adding the two 16th/8th-rest rhythm.
2. In this chapter, the beats are slower. You can play them faster, but they are designed to help you learn slow grooves like Led Zeppelin's "When the Levee Breaks," with John Bonham on the drums.
3. MM = 76-80.

Warm-Up

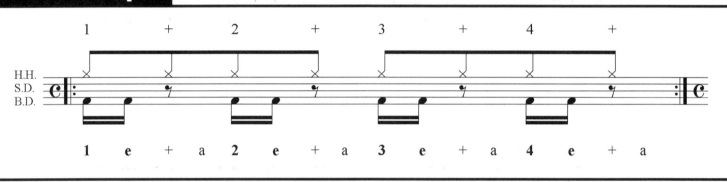

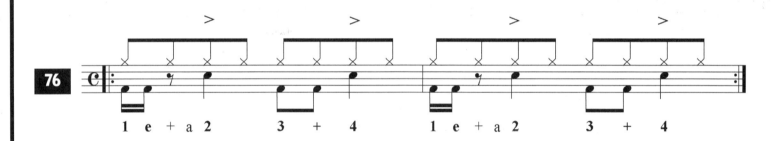

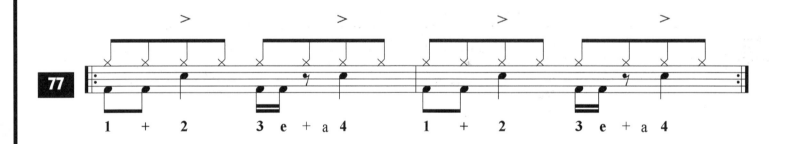

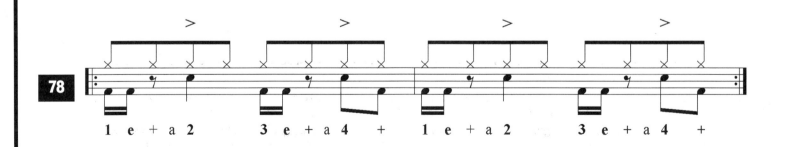

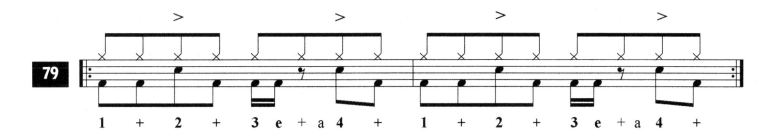

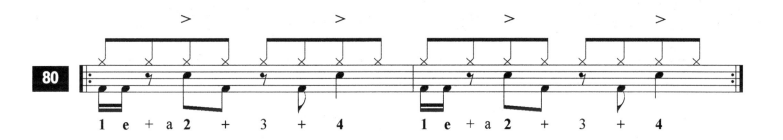

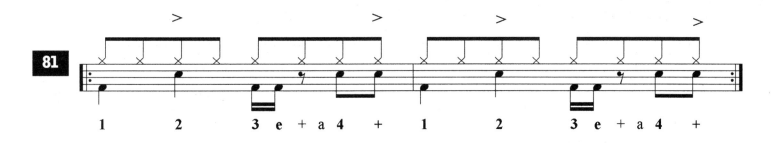

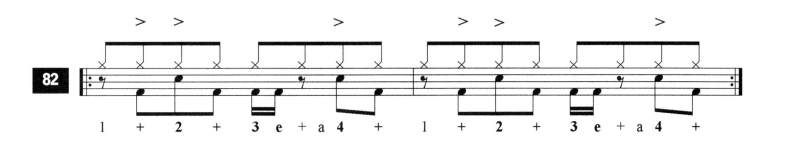

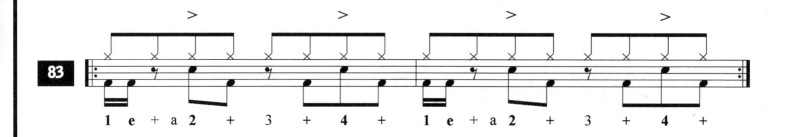

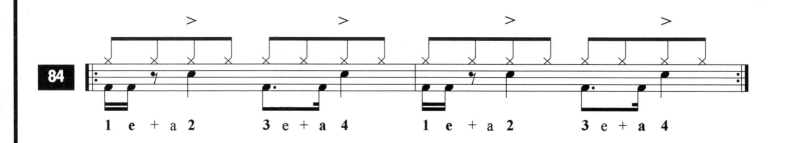

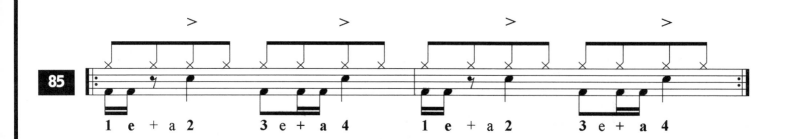

CHAPTER SEVEN
Syncopated 16th-Note Rhythmic Pattern

1. Adding sixteenth/eighth/sixteenth rhythm.
2. MM marking = 100-120.

Warm-Up

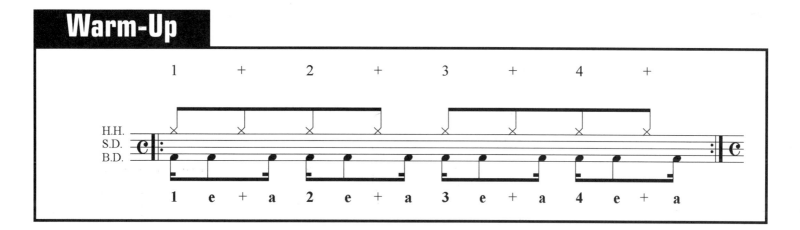

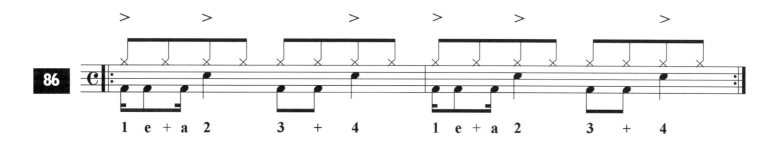

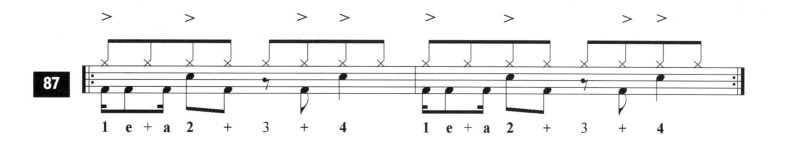

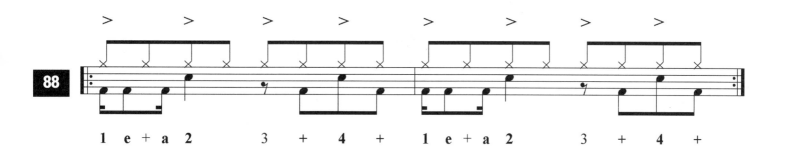

89

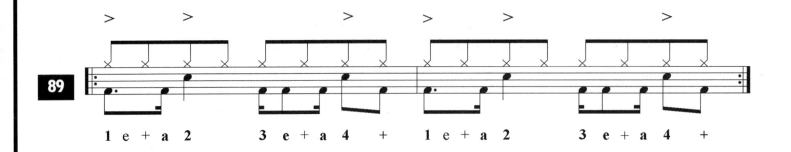

1 e + a 2   3 e + a 4 + 1 e + a 2   3 e + a 4 +

90

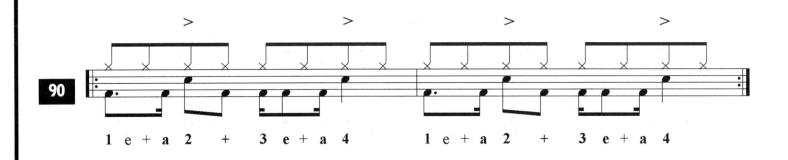

1 e + a 2 + 3 e + a 4 1 e + a 2 + 3 e + a 4

91

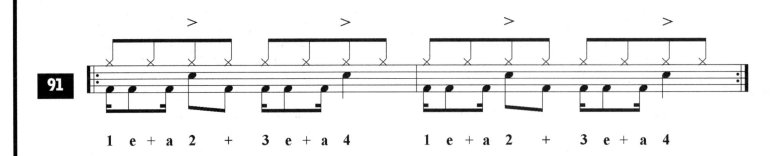

1 e + a 2 + 3 e + a 4 1 e + a 2 + 3 e + a 4

92

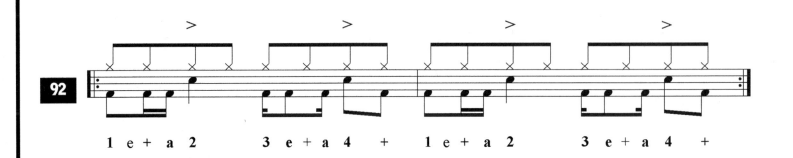

1 e + a 2   3 e + a 4 + 1 e + a 2   3 e + a 4 +

93

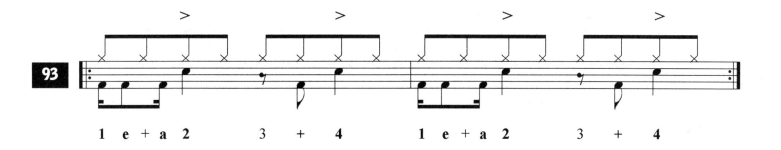

1 e + a 2   3 + 4   1 e + a 2   3 + 4

94

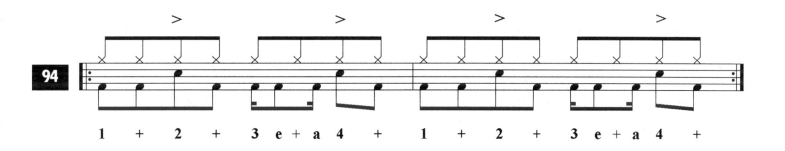

1 + 2 + 3 e + a 4 +   1 + 2 + 3 e + a 4 +

95

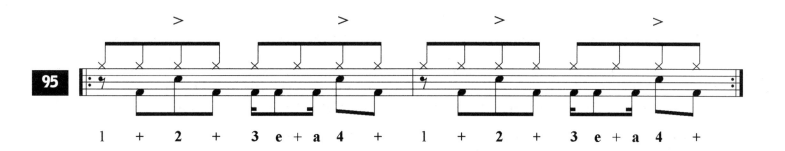

1 + 2 + 3 e + a 4 +   1 + 2 + 3 e + a 4 +

CHAPTER EIGHT
16th-Note Variations with Rests

1. Adding 16th rest/two 16th-notes/16th-rest rhythm.
2. MM marking = 88-120.

Warm-Up

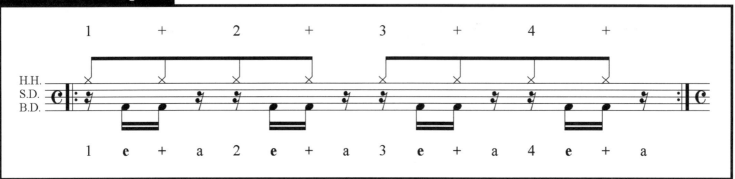

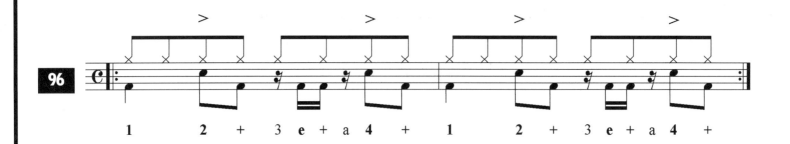

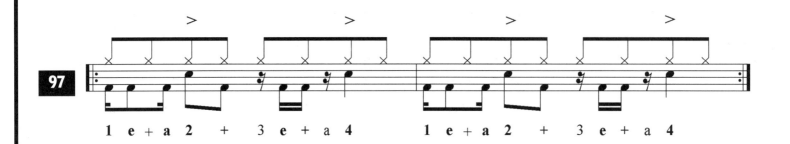

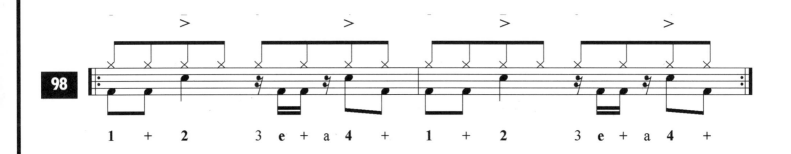

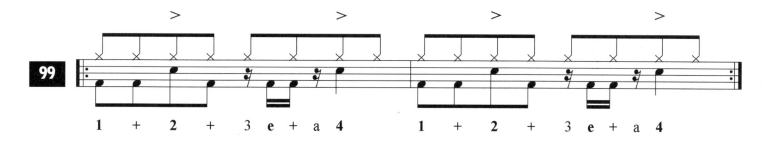

99

1 + 2 + 3 e + a 4   1 + 2 + 3 e + a 4

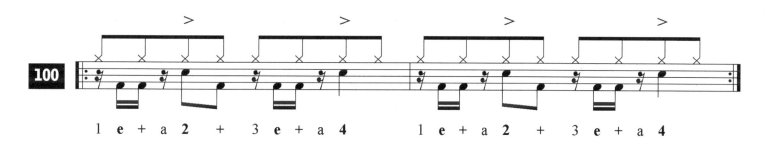

100

1 e + a 2 + 3 e + a 4   1 e + a 2 + 3 e + a 4

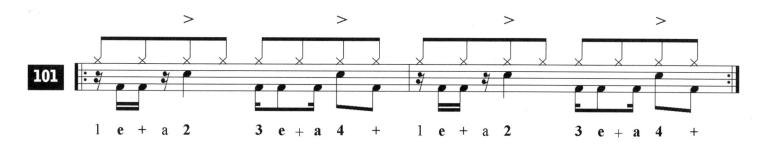

101

1 e + a 2   3 e + a 4 +   1 e + a 2   3 e + a 4 +

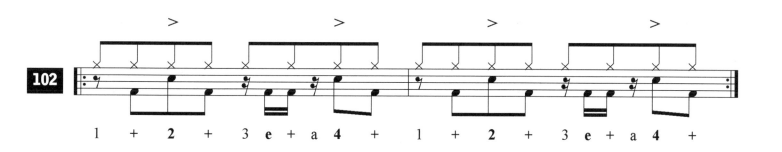

102

1 + 2 + 3 e + a 4 +   1 + 2 + 3 e + a 4 +

103

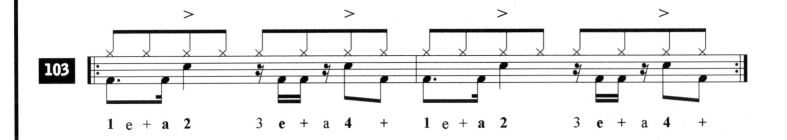

1 e + a 2   3 e + a 4 +   1 e + a 2   3 e + a 4 +

104

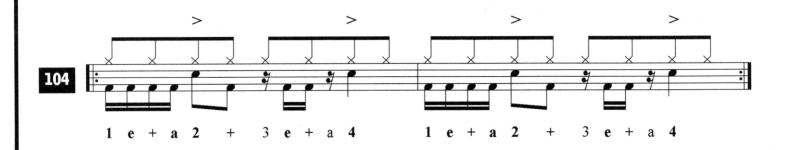

1 e + a 2 + 3 e + a 4   1 e + a 2 + 3 e + a 4

105

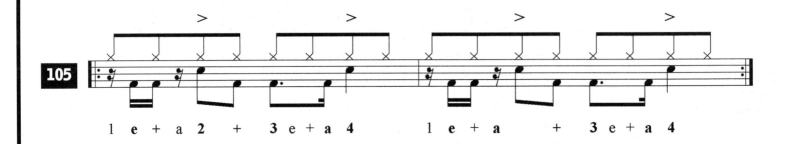

1 e + a 2 + 3 e + a 4   1 e + a   + 3 e + a 4

CHAPTER NINE
Putting It All Together with Ghost Notes

1. Adding alternating 16th-rest/16th-note rhythm.
2. Mixing rhythms from chapters 1-8.
3. Adding more snare drum notes.
4. Notes in ( ) are played as soft ghost notes. Play these ghost notes no more than 1/2" from the head.
5. MM marking: whatever feels comfortable.

Warm-Up

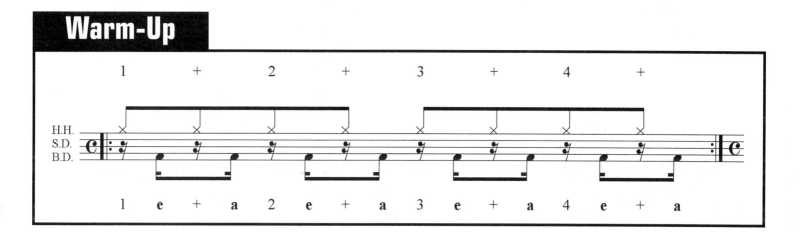

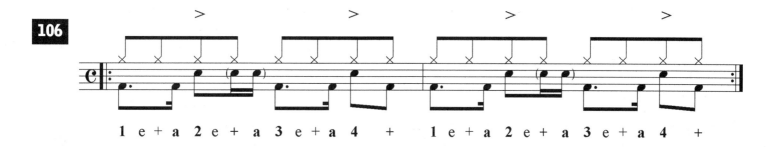

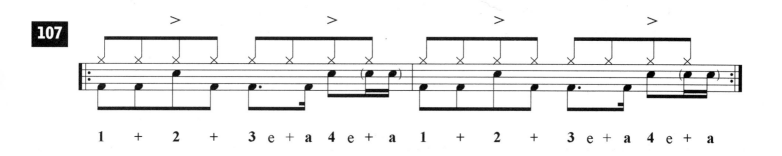

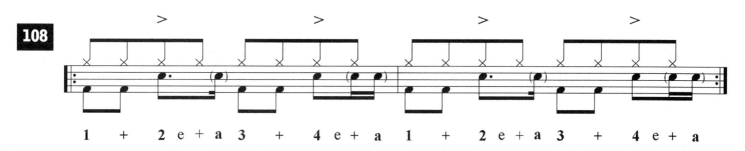

109

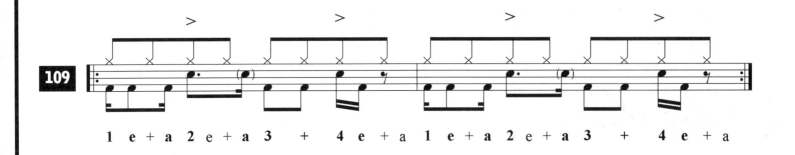

1 e + a 2 e + a 3 + 4 e + a 1 e + a 2 e + a 3 + 4 e + a

110

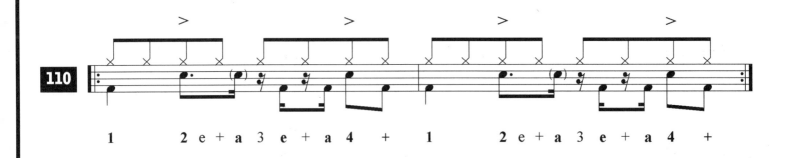

1 2 e + a 3 e + a 4 + 1 2 e + a 3 e + a 4 +

111

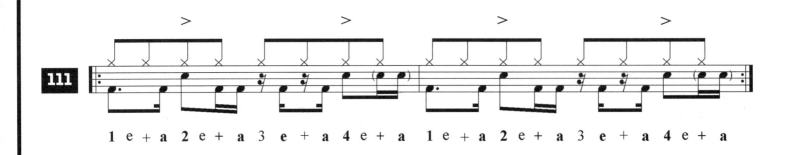

1 e + a 2 e + a 3 e + a 4 e + a 1 e + a 2 e + a 3 e + a 4 e + a

112

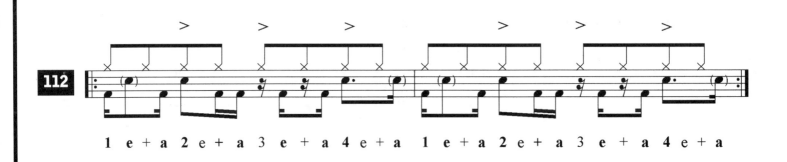

1 e + a 2 e + a 3 e + a 4 e + a 1 e + a 2 e + a 3 e + a 4 e + a

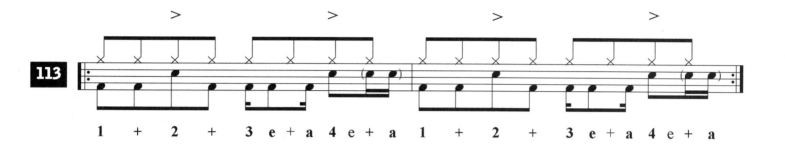

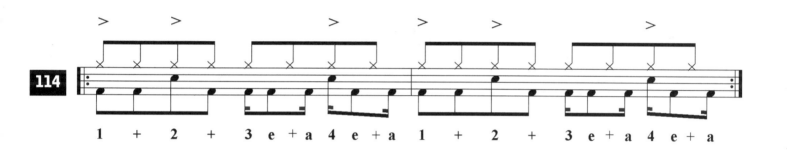

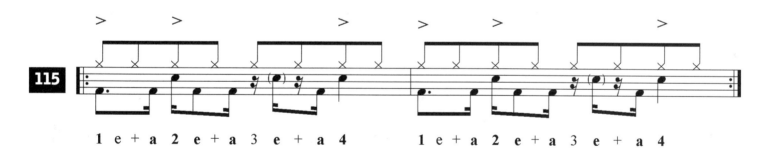

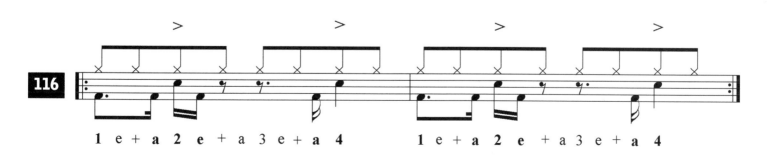

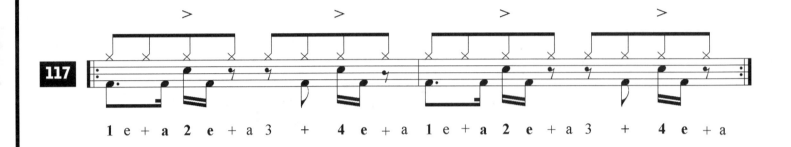

117

1 e + a 2 e + a 3 + 4 e + a 1 e + a 2 e + a 3 + 4 e + a

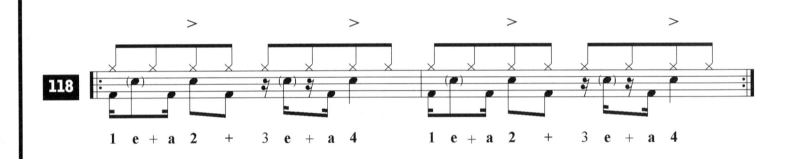

118

1 e + a 2 + 3 e + a 4 1 e + a 2 + 3 e + a 4

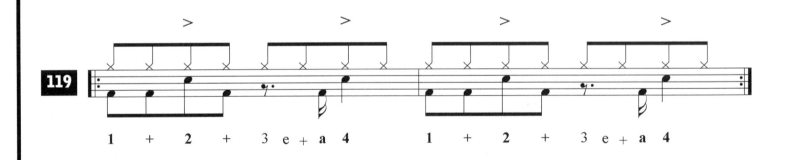

119

1 + 2 + 3 e + a 4 1 + 2 + 3 e + a 4

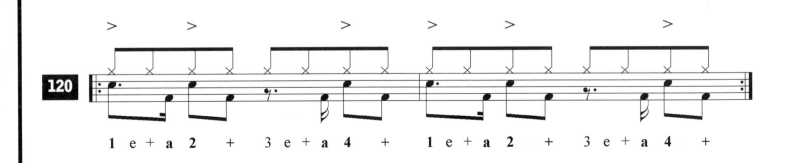

120

1 e + a 2 + 3 e + a 4 + 1 e + a 2 + 3 e + a 4 +

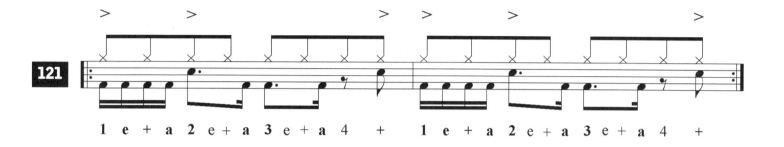

121

1 e + a 2 e + a 3 e + a 4   +   1 e + a 2 e + a 3 e + a 4   +

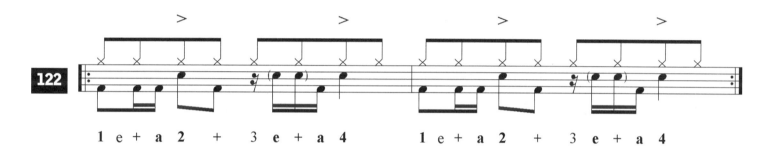

122

1 e + a 2   +   3 e + a 4   1 e + a 2   +   3 e + a 4

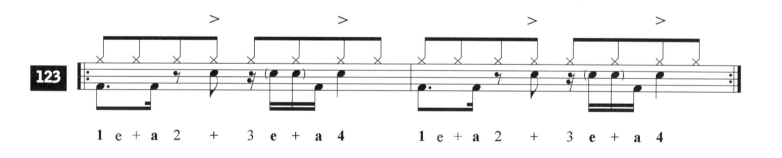

123

1 e + a 2   +   3 e + a 4   1 e + a 2   +   3 e + a 4

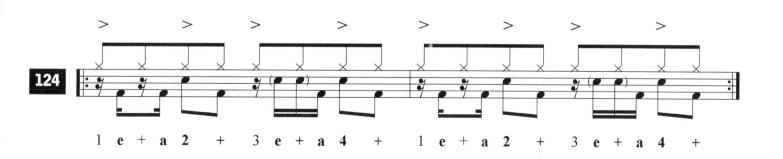

124

1 e + a 2   +   3 e + a 4   +   1 e + a 2   +   3 e + a 4   +

125

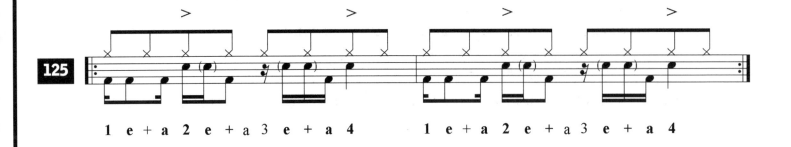

1 e + a 2 e + a 3 e + a 4   1 e + a 2 e + a 3 e + a 4

126

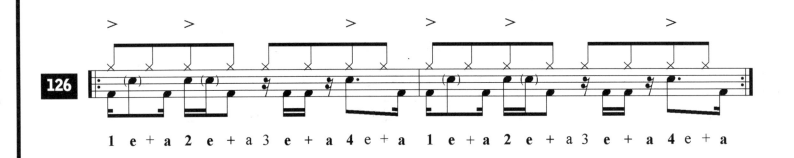

1 e + a 2 e + a 3 e + a 4 e + a 1 e + a 2 e + a 3 e + a 4 e + a

127

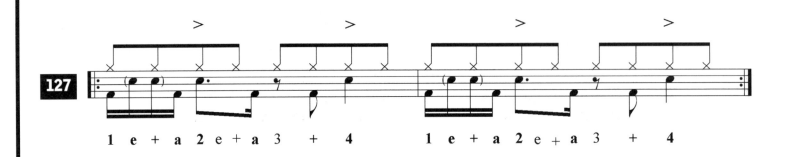

1 e + a 2 e + a 3 + 4   1 e + a 2 e + a 3 + 4

128

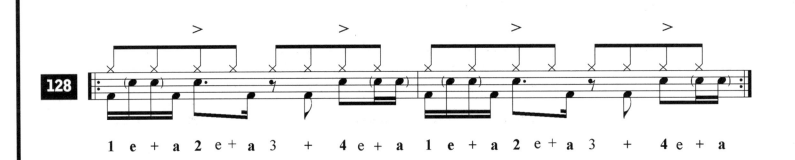

1 e + a 2 e + a 3 + 4 e + a 1 e + a 2 e + a 3 + 4 e + a

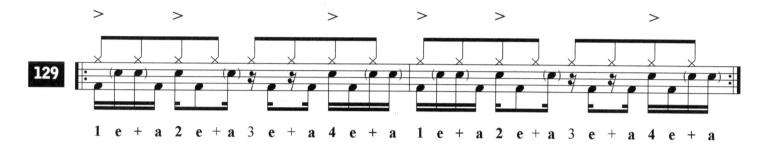

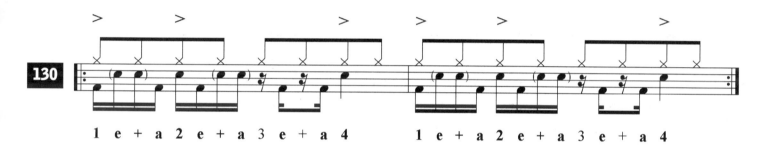

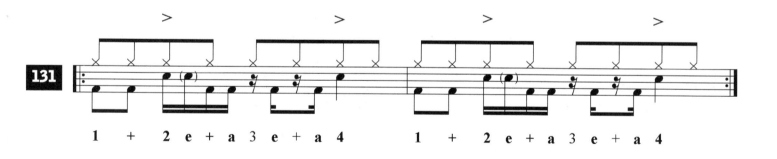

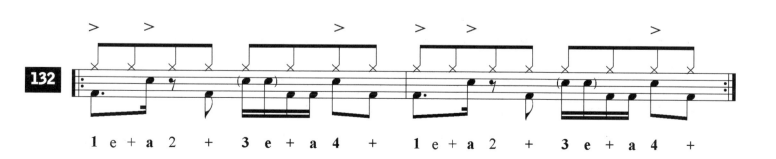

133

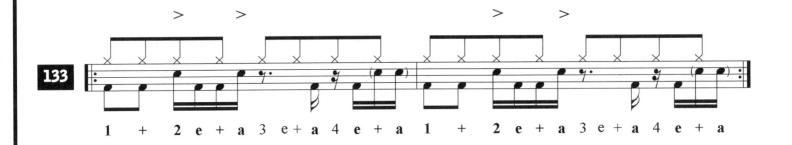

1 + 2 e + a 3 e + a 4 e + a 1 + 2 e + a 3 e + a 4 e + a

134

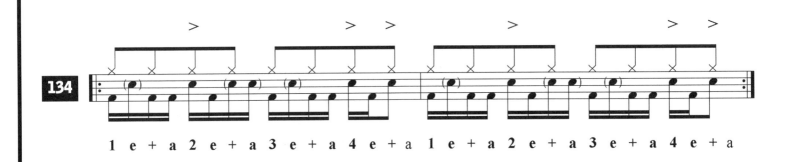

1 e + a 2 e + a 3 e + a 4 e + a 1 e + a 2 e + a 3 e + a 4 e + a

135

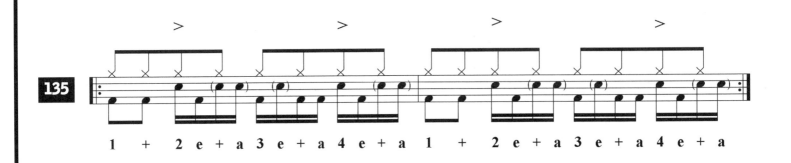

1 + 2 e + a 3 e + a 4 e + a 1 + 2 e + a 3 e + a 4 e + a

136

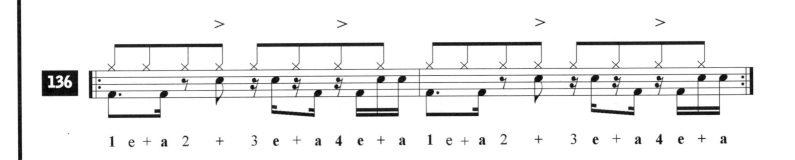

1 e + a 2 + 3 e + a 4 e + a 1 e + a 2 + 3 e + a 4 e + a

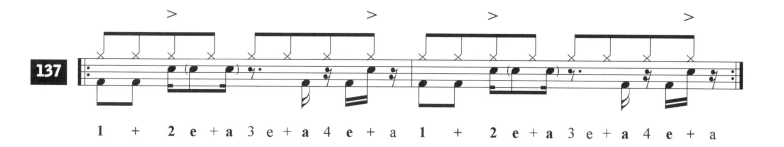

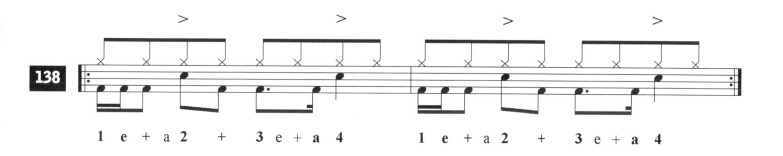

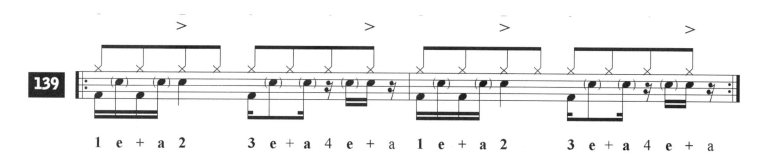

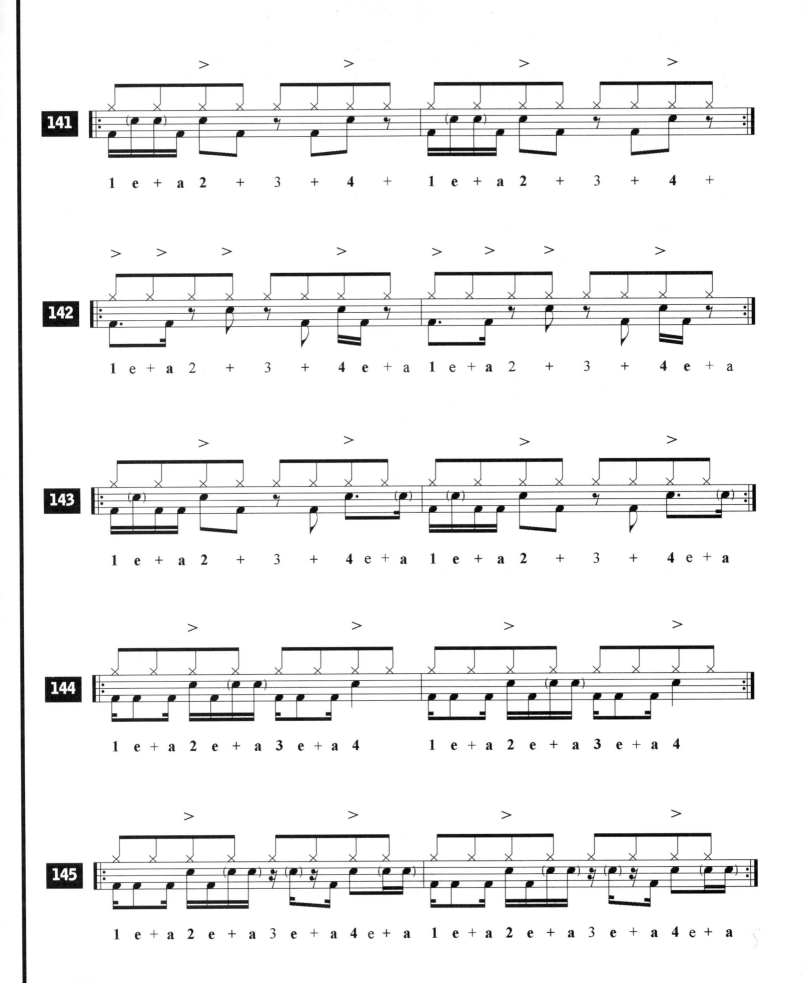

APPENDIX

Suggested Materials for Further Study:

Beginner-Intermediate Snare Drum Studies
Alfred's Drum Method, Volume 1, by Sandy Feldstein and Dave Black—Alfred Publishing Co.
Alfred's Drum Method, Volume 2, by Sandy Feldstein and Dave Black—Alfred Publishing Co.
Breeze-Easy Method 1, Drums, by John Kinyon—Alfred Publishing Co.
Breeze-Easy Method 2, Drums, by John Kinyon—Alfred Publishing Co.
Elementary Drum Method, by Roy Burns—Alfred Publishing Co.
Progressive Steps to Syncopation for the Modern Drummer, by Ted Reed—Alfred Publishing Co.

Hand Technique Studies
Stick Control, by George Lawrence Stone—George B. Stone & Son, Inc.
Accents and Rebounds, by George Lawrence Stone—George B. Stone & Son, Inc.
Master Studies, by Joe Morello—Modern Drummer Publications, Inc.
It's Your Move: Motions and Emotions, by Dom Famularo, with Joe Bergamini—Alfred Publishing Co.

Intermediate-Advanced Snare Drum Studies
Podemski's Standard Snare Drum Method, by Benjamin Podemski—Alfred Publishing Co.
Contemporary Studies for the Snare Drum, by Fred Albright—Alfred Publishing Co.
Portraits in Rhythm, by Anthony J. Cirone—Alfred Publishing Co.

Rudimental Snare Studies
Savage Rudimental Workshop, by Matt Savage— Alfred Publishing Co.
America's N.A.R.D. Drum Solos—Ludwig Music Publishing Co.
Modern Rudimental Swing Solos, by Charley Wilcoxon—Ludwig Music Publishing Co.
Rudiments & Motions: Snare Drumming Up Close, by Frank Corniola—Musos Publications PTY.LTD

Beginning-Intermediate Drumset Studies
Getting Started on Drums, by Tommy Igoe—Hal Leonard Corp.
Elementary Rock and Roll Drumming, by Roy Burns and Howard Halpern—Alfred Publishing Co.
Alfred's Beginning Drumset Method, by Sandy Feldstein and Dave Black—Alfred Publishing Co.
Rockin' Bass Drum 1 and 2, by John Lombardo and Charles Perry—Alfred Publishing Co.
Updated Realistic Rock Drum Method, by Carmine Appice—Alfred Publishing Co.
Building Blocks of Rock, by Dawn Richardson—Mel Bay Publications

Intermediate-Advanced Drumset Studies
MD Classic Tracks: The World's Greatest Drummers, by Joe Bergamini—Modern Drummer Publications
Drum Techniques of Led Zeppelin, by Joe Bergamini—Alfred Publishing Co.
Operation: Rockenfield, by Joe Bergamini and Craig LeMay—Carl Fischer.
Drumming Out Of The Shadows, by Jason Bittner, Joe Bergamini & Willie Rose—Carl Fischer.
Advanced Funk Studies, by Rick Latham—Rick Latham Publishing Co. / Carl Fischer
Future Sounds, by David Garibaldi—Alfred Publishing Co.
The New Breed, by Gary Chester—Modern Drummer Publications, Inc.
The Funky Beat, by David Garibaldi—Alfred Publishing Co.
TimbaFunk, by David Garibaldi & Talking Drums—Alfred Publishing Co.
Contemporary Drummer + One, by Dave Weckl—Alfred Publishing Co.

APPENDIX
(CONTINUED)

Bass Drum Technique Studies
Progressive Steps to Bass Drum Technique, by Ted Reed—Alfred Publishing Co.
Bass Drum Control, by Colin Bailey—Hal Leonard Corp.
Bass Drum Essentials for the Drumset, by Dave Black and Brian Fullen—Alfred Publishing Co.

Recommended Videos
Led Zeppelin: Led Zeppelin; M: Productions; John Bonham.
PAS Larrie Londin Benefit Concert; Various Artists; Alfred Publishing Co.
AUDW 2002/2003/2004; Various Artists; Hudson Music.
Steve Smith: Drumset Technique/History of the U.S. Beat; Steve Smith; Hudson Music.
Jim Chapin: Speed, Power, Control, Endurance; Jim Chapin; Alfred Publishing Co.
Zildjian Presents: The New A Customs; Vinnie Colaiuta; Avedis Zildjian Company.
Gregg Bissonette: Private Lesson; Gregg Bissonette; Alfred Publishing Co.
John Blackwell: Technique, Grooving and Showmanship; John Blackwell; Hudson Music.
A Salute to Buddy Rich; Phil Collins, Dennis Chambers, and Steve Smith; Hudson Music.
Drummers Collective: 25th Anniversary Celebration and Bass Day 2002; Various Artists; Hudson Music.
Steve Gadd: In Session; Steve Gadd; Alfred Publishing Co.
Tower of Groove (1 & 2), Talking Drums; David Garibaldi; Alfred Publishing Co.
The Natural Approach to Technique; Joe Morello; Hot Licks.
Billy Cobham: Drums By Design; Billy Cobham; Alfred Publishing Co.
Will Kennedy: Be A Drumhead; Will Kennedy; Alfred Publishing Co.
Bobby Rock: Metalmorphosis; Bobby Rock; Alfred Publishing Co.
Carter Beauford and Victor Wooten: Making Music; Hudson Music.
Tommy Igoe: Getting Started on Drums; Hal Leonard Corp.
Simon Phillips: Drum Tips; Alfred Publishing Co.

ACKNOWLEDGEMENTS

Thank You:

Paul Ceglia, for encouraging me to take up drumming and for being a lifetime drumming buddy.

Johnny Blowers, for teaching many styles of music and sharing your love of drumming.

Ronnie Gould, for sharing your knowledge of hand technique, mallet and timpani playing.

Charlie Perry, for expanding hand technique to drumset.

Mel Davis, for letting me play at Mel's Place with him, and teaching me how to really play set with a band.

Jim Peterscak, for expanding my repertoire and leading me toward teaching. "You did good, J.P.!"

Dom Famularo, for opening the box and teaching me the big techniques. Your playing, teaching, and energy are always an inspiration to me.

Steve Leahy, for sharing your artistic talent and creating the fantastic cover drawing.

Amanda Grimaldi, for your dedication and endless effort transcribing this book on Finale.

DCS Students, for providing the inspiration for this book.

A special thanks to my wife, Shelley,
for always encouraging me to move ahead.
To my son, Chris, a great young person—
thanks for jamming with the old guy.
To my late mother, Lorraine:
Without your love and support I would not have made it.